G-FAAW

R101

A PICTORIAL HISTORY

NICK LE NEVE WALMSLEY

SUTTON PUBLISHING

First published in the United Kingdom in 2000 by
Sutton Publishing Limited · Phoenix Mill
Thrupp · Stroud · Gloucestershire · GL5 2BU

British Library Cataloguing in Publication Data
A catalogue record for this book is available from the British Library.

ISBN 0-7509-2502-7

For 'Jim' and the lads

Typeset in 11/14pt Photina.
Typesetting and origination by
Sutton Publishing Limited.
Printed and bound in England by
J.H. Haynes & Co. Ltd, Sparkford.

Contents

A pin-sharp image of the 'factory-fresh' R101 riding at the mast head following her emergence from Cardington's No. 1 Shed on 12 October 1929.

Foreword

Current air travel, with long-haul flights, is so very much a feature of modern times that earlier aerial endeavour tends to be forgotten. After all, even in the 1950s trans-Atlantic crossings made use of Newfoundland or the Azores, with the ocean too broad for direct and regular passage between Europe and the United States.

No wonder we can forget that plans took shape eight decades ago to connect distant portions of the British Empire by extremely long-haul airship flights. Not only would these journeys be far swifter than any ship's passage but very much quicker than heavy aircraft were able to achieve, with their frequent need for fuel. Even more to the point, as Nevil Shute phrased it, their passengers would eat meals and sleep at night 'in a Christian manner', unlike today's devilish and cramped aircraft confinement.

Ill-fortune then killed Britain's airship programme, but *R101 – A Pictorial History* can help us relive that former dream. We of the Airship Heritage Trust (formerly Friends of Cardington Airship Station) are doing our best to keep such memories alive, and will be establishing a great museum before too long. Without doubt this excellent and timely book will be at the forefront of our wares for sale.

Anthony Smith
Chairman, Airship Heritage Trust

This peaceful pastoral scene of R101, dating from October 1929, seems a world away from the horrors that were to befall her a year later.

Preface

'R100 gave me pleasure. R101 will, I hope, give me joy. To ride the storm has always been my ambition and who knows but we may realise it on the way to India – but not, I hope, with undue risk to human lives.'

Lord Thomson of Cardington, letter to Marthe Lucie, the Princess Bibesco, 20 August 1930.

'There are two tragedies in life. One is not to get your heart's desire. The other is – to get it.'

George Bernard Shaw, *Man and Superman*

Those quotes sum up the entire story of R101 and the personalities who moved within her orbit. They preface what might be called the modern R101 'bible' – *To Ride the Storm* was written by Sir Peter G. Masefield and published in 1982, the fruit of a lifetime connected with the aeronautical world, coupled with a passion for airships. Every modern commentator on R101 cannot help but acknowledge a debt to Sir Peter's monumental work, whether they question or endorse his views. This present book is no exception, and its aim is simple: to attempt a pictorial history of R101 in contemporary photographs to complement the millions of words written about her since the late 1920s. The selection of the photographs – a daunting task in itself - is a personal one designed to interest the casual reader and R101 *aficionado* alike. There are omissions, yes: but the airship book which is concise, complete and faultless has yet to be written!

The photographs are all taken from original prints which are owned by the Airship Heritage Trust, and which form part of their unique archives currently housed in the grounds of Shuttleworth College at Old Warden in Bedfordshire; the text is drawn from oral accounts, manuscript and printed sources, official reports and contemporary press items in the same archive. All the images are over seventy years old; many were literally saved from the bonfires that followed the break-up of the old Royal Airship Works; others are from photographers and photo agencies long vanished and some have been loaned from family albums. Whilst every effort has been made to trace possible copyright holders, the frequent presence of identical photographs in more than one archive and the common difficulty of tracing the original provenance of an illustration seventy or eighty years on means that unwitting mistakes may have been made in attribution, for which the author apologises. It is thus in this spirit of good faith that the Airship Heritage Trust has been happy to make available these largely unseen treasures from its archive for enjoyment by a wider audience.

Nick le Neve Walmsley
Hoveton St John, July 2000

Acknowledgements

To the following, for the loan of material, help, encouragement, patience and friendship, I am deeply indebted: Den Burchmore; Group Capt. Peter Garth; Norman Peake and Anthony Smith of the Airship Heritage Trust; Group Capt. and Mrs. E.A. Johnston; Sir Peter G. Masefield; Crispin Rope; Mrs Doreen Rope; Patrick Abbott; Philip Armes; Mrs Mary Atkinson; Henry Ayres; Don Beattie; Jeanne Burchmore; Jim Colman (Boulton and Paul, Norwich); John Christopher; Mrs Beryl Critchell; Ray Dudley; John Duggan; Mrs Emily Jane Earle; Simon Fletcher (Sutton Publishing); the late Ted Greenstreet; Mrs Enid Holmes; Albert Hunt; Mrs Ina James; Alastair Lawson; Arnold Nayler (Royal Aeronautical Society); Stewart Orr (Radio Norfolk); Steve Snelling (Eastern Counties Newspapers); Mr and Mrs Peter Walmsley; Laurent Wattebled; and all the other members of the extended R101 'family'.

Introduction

Britain's airship fleet had been decommissioned after the Great War, as the Air Ministry felt the way ahead lay with aeroplanes. But in 1922 the energetic and influential Commander Dennistoun Burney, Conservative MP for Uxbridge, proposed that it would be strategically desirable for Britain to have a fleet of long-range airships which could connect far-flung corners of the Empire in a fraction of the time it took to make a sea voyage. Aeroplanes were still primitive, cramped and uncomfortable then, and needed frequent stops too; but airships were the liners of the skies, able to move passengers, freight – and troops – in relative comfort and luxury without the need to stop for at least forty-eight hours.

Cardington, centrally placed in the country, was provisionally designated to be the hub of the operation, the Heathrow of its day. Although the Conservative Government under Lloyd George was initially sceptical, under the influence of Sir Samuel Hoare (later Lord Templewood) it gradually embraced the idea of Burney's fast Empire routes, and in the spirit of private enterprise Vickers Ltd were given a franchise to build six airships for the Britain to India route. This was the origin of R100. The general election which produced the first Labour government early in 1924 threw everything into the melting pot, but the new Minister for Air, the cultured and charismatic Brigadier-General Christopher Birdwood Thomson, gave his complete backing to the scheme, even taking the title 'Lord Thomson of Cardington' on his elevation to the Cabinet. He knew that the French airship *Dixmude* and her Commander, Jean du Plessis de Grenedan, had proved that Mother Countries and their outposts could be linked by airship, and that America was building the first of her long-range rigid airships too. The loss of *Dixmude* with all hands nine months earlier should not be seen as a deterrent: 'Britain must not stand idly by', he said and thus, early in 1924, the Government-funded R101 programme came into being. The supposed rivalry between the 'Capitalist' ship (R100) and the 'Socialist' Ship (R101) was readily exploited by the popular press.

Some preliminary testing on the viability of large rigid airships as rapid transport across the Empire had already been carried out in the aftermath of the Great War using British-built Zeppelin 'copies' R33, R34 and R36. In July 1919 R34 had flown the Atlantic, both ways, in a fraction of the time it took to make a sea crossing; in so doing she became the first aircraft ever to make a double crossing of the Atlantic from mainland to mainland – a fact which is all to conveniently forgotten by the promotors of aeroplanes who continue to champion Alcock and Brown as being the first across! Under the command of Major Herbert Scott, R34 caused a sensation on both sides of the Atlantic, especially following the discovery of two stowaways – a young rigger and his tabby kitten – on the outward leg of the journey. The programme continued with the first purpose-built British passenger rigid airship, R36; although a beautiful ship, she was doomed to have a very short service life. She was severely damaged in a mooring accident at the experimental high mooring mast at Pulham in Norfolk, and subsequently broken up; but not before she had carried out flights of great duration – and had been used by the Metropolitan Police to direct traffic at the 1921 Royal Ascot race meeting, the first recorded instance of an airborne police traffic control post, kept in touch by wireless with officers on the ground. The press were also able to write their copy aboard her that day, and see it dropped by parachute to be whisked away to Fleet Street by motorcycle courier! It all caused a good deal of excitement, and was still fresh in the mind when Commander Dennistoun Burney proposed his great Imperial British Airship Programme in 1922.

CHAPTER ONE

The Driving Personalities

The men behind the Government's British Airship Programme of 1924–30 photographed before boarding R101 at Cardington, 4 October 1930: in the centre, Lord Thomson of Cardington, Secretary of State for Air; to the right, Lt. Col. Vincent Richmond, Assistant Director of Airship Development (Technical), the chief designer of R101; and Sir Sefton Brancker, Director of Civil Aviation, with his trademark rimless monocle. On the extreme left is Sqn. Ldr. Ernest Johnston, R101's navigator. All were killed at Allonne, except for Major Louis Reynolds, the figure in the bowler hat; he was principal assistant to Lord Thomson but did not travel on the ship.

Brigadier-General the Right Honourable the Lord Thomson of Cardington (1875–1930), Minister for Air in the first Labour Government in Britain. He inherited the idea of the Imperial Airship Service from his Conservative predecessor, Sir Samuel Hoare, and became its chief advocate. He was an ambitious politician who had his eye on becoming Viceroy of India – it was mainly owing to his insistence that he should arrive at the October 1930 Imperial Conference in India by airship that R101 was rushed through her trials with indecent haste.

Wing Commander Reginald Colmore (1887–1930), Director of Airship Development, had been connected with airship design since the Great War and, whilst a great believer in airships, was also aware of their limitations. Colmore was the head of the triangle that formed Cardington's 'Big Three' with Richmond and Scott.

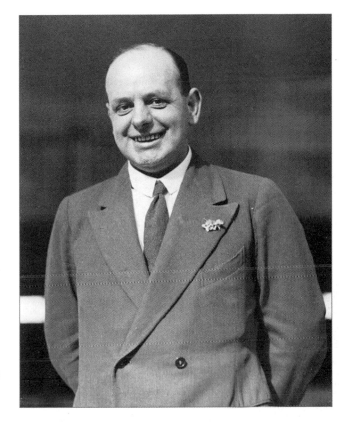

Major G.H. Scott (1888–1930), Assistant Director of Airship Development (Flying), was a man touched by genius, a vastly experienced veteran airshipman, and the pioneer of the high mast system of mooring airships. His pilot's licence was 'British Airship Pilot No. A1 (First Class)'; he had commanded No. 9, the first successful British rigid airship; and he had been in charge of R34 on her trailblazing double crossing of the Atlantic in July 1919. As director of the airship station at Pulham in Norfolk, he had been responsible for the experimental work leading up to the Government Airship programme of 1924.

Lord Thomson greeting Major Scott at the base of the Cardington mooring mast in August 1930, after R100's transatlantic flight to Canada. Scott had been Officer in Charge on that flight.

Sqn. Ldr. Michael Rope (1888–1930), the brilliant designer who assisted Richmond. Many of the effective technical advances built into R101 came from his fertile mind. Like all the main players in the R101 story he had enjoyed distinguished service in airships during the Great War, and had designed the outstanding SS Zero non-rigid airship for convoy protection duties. Described as 'a modest and retiring genius', few realised how gifted and valuable he was to the whole R101 project.

Scott with Sqn. Ldr. Ernest Johnston (1891–1930), a brilliant navigator and first Master of the new Livery Guild of Air Pilots and Navigators who, accompanied by Sir Samuel Hoare, had surveyed the routes down to India that the new fleet of airships was to follow. Johnston had served on the RNAS airships in the Great War and was highly experienced.

Harold Roxbee Cox (1902–97), seen here in later life as Lord King's Norton, was the Chief Calculator of R101, responsible for calculating stresses within the airframe.

R101 was the first airship to use high tensile steel in its construction: this had a greater weight/strength ratio than duralumin. John Dudley North (1893–1968), a pioneer of metal aircraft construction and the Chief Designer of Boulton and Paul Aircraft, was brought in to advise on construction and, as a most ingenious engineer, he worked closely with Richmond and his assistant Michael Rope. All the girderwork was sub-contracted to Boulton and Paul who made the framework of R101 at their works in Norwich.

The staff of the Drawing Office at the Royal Airship Works (RAW) pictured in the Headquarters Building at Cardington in the 1920s. They were responsible for turning the vision of the great ship into technical drawings and building blueprints. Some 270 staff were engaged on design alone, with another 700 employed on construction at Norwich and Cardington.

CHAPTER TWO

Constructing R101

Draughtsman Cracknell of the Cardington Drawing Office gave an early impression (1926) of how HMA R101 would look in RAF service. The 1924 specification had called for an airship of not less than 5,000,000 cubic feet capacity, not weighing more than 90 tons, yet being capable of cruising at 63 mph for forty-eight hours whilst carrying 100 passengers. It was also envisaged that the airship would be able to carry two or more scouting aircraft.

A rigid airship is basically a lot of balloons (gas bags) filled with lighter-than-air gas to give lift, and held together with an external rigid framework. The gas bags must be made of gas-proof material, and the framework covered with linen to protect them. The form had been pioneered by Count Ferdinand von Zeppelin in Germany at the turn of the century. Big rigid airships can carry large numbers of passengers and freight, either below their hulls or within them. R101 was conceived as a beautifully streamlined ship with her accommodation inside the hull, along with the gas bags.

As America had a monopoly on helium (a safe, inert lifting gas), the only alternative open to R101's designers was the highly inflammable hydrogen (a much better lifting agent than helium, however). In order to lift both the weight of the airship, and a realistic payload, it was calculated that a volume of 5,000,000 cubic feet of hydrogen would be needed, making a huge airship 732 ft long and 132 ft in diameter. R101 was the largest flying object ever built when she was launched in 1929. As the following pictures show, R101 began as a gigantic Meccano set. She was new in every sense, embodying many design innovations – perhaps too many all at once. The rival Airship Guarantee Company (Vickers) at Howden in Yorkshire, was playing safe: their R100 was being designed by Barnes Wallis, but built with tried and tested Zeppelin technology developed by Germany in the Great War.

Opposite, overleaf and page 12: When the Press was allowed to visit R101 on 2 October 1929, *Illustrated London News* artist G.H. Davis prepared some artist's impressions for readers. His sketches give a vivid impression of the luxurious appointment of the airship, even if his idea of scale throughout the ship is generous where headroom is concerned! The passengers would have enjoyed all the comforts expected on an ocean liner of the time even if the materials used were not so solid: the 'walls' were actually of canvas, and the solid-looking columns were duralumin with balsa-wood cladding. There was even an airtight smoking room, where cigarettes could be enjoyed in close proximity to 5,000,000 cubic feet of highly inflammable hydrogen!

Smoking Room.

Typical
Two-Berth Cabin.
Electric Light.
← Blind.
Steel Tube.
Curtain.

Main Staircase.

Metal floor to prevent
any chance of fire from
carelessly thrown down
matches or cigarettes.

Corridor.

Heating
Ventila
Grati

Starboard Promenade Deck.

Lounge.

Cellon Windows.

Unsplinterable
Glass Windows.

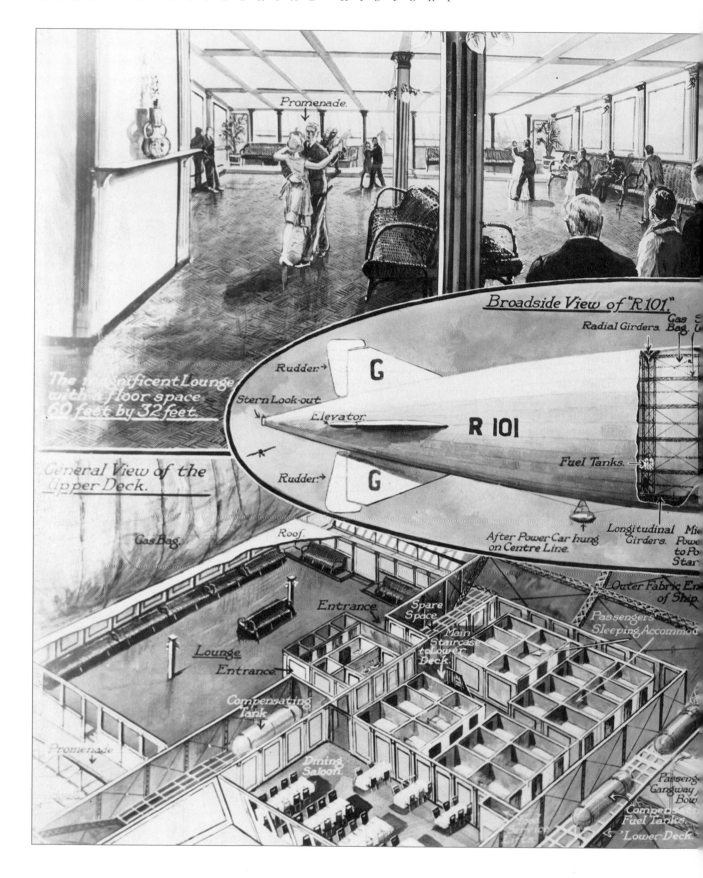

Promenade.

The magnificent Lounge with a floor space 60 feet by 32 feet.

General View of the Upper Deck.

Broadside View of "R101."

Radial Girders. Gas Bag.

Rudder. G

Stern Look-out

Elevator. R 101

Rudder. G

Fuel Tanks.

After Power Car hung on Centre Line.

Longitudinal Girders.

Gas Bag.

Roof.

Entrance.

Spare Space

Main Staircase to Lower Deck.

Outer Fabric End of Ship.

Passengers' Sleeping Accommod

Lounge Entrance.

Compensating Tank

Promenade.

Dining Saloon.

Passeng Gangway Bow

Compens Fuel Tanks. Lower Deck.

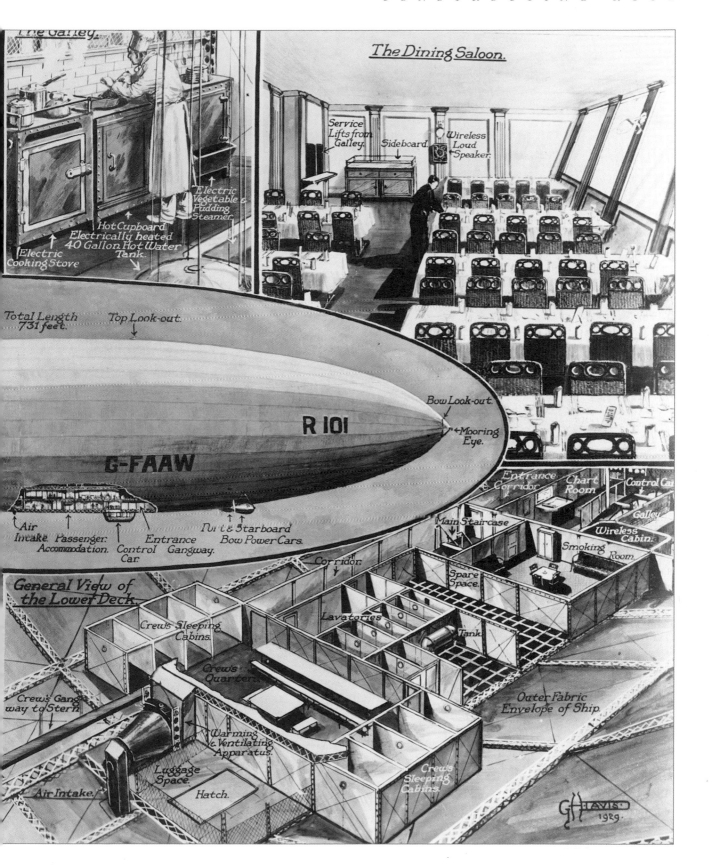

The Galley.

The Dining Saloon.

Service Lifts from Galley.

Sideboard.

Wireless Loud Speaker.

Electric Vegetable & Pudding Steamer.

Hot Cupboard Electrically heated 40 Gallon Hot Water Tank.

Electric Cooking Stove

Total Length 731 feet.

Top Look-out.

Bow Look-out.

Mooring Eye.

R 101

G-FAAW

Air Intake. Passenger Accommodation.

Entrance Control Car.

Port & Starboard Bow Power Cars.

Entrance Gangway.

Entrance Corridor.

Chart Room.

Control Car.

Galley.

Main Staircase.

Wireless Cabin.

Smoking Room.

Corridor.

Spare Space.

General View of the Lower Deck.

Crew's Sleeping Cabins.

Lavatories.

Tank.

Crew's Quarters.

Crew's Gang way to Stern.

Outer Fabric Envelope of Ship.

Warming & Ventilating Apparatus.

Luggage Space.

Hatch.

Crew's Sleeping Cabins.

Air Intake.

G H DAVIS 1929.

11

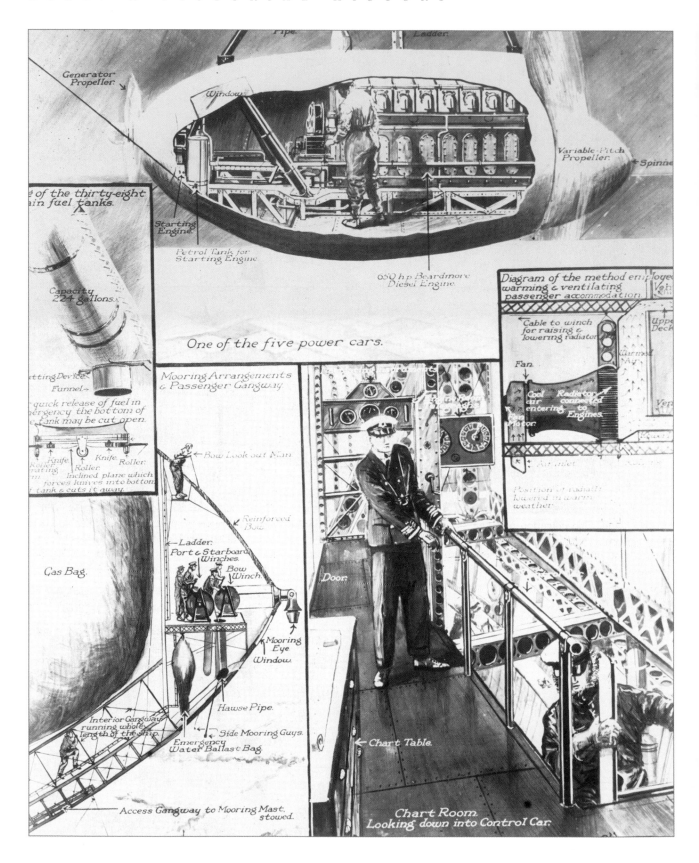

Generator Propeller.

Variable-Pitch Propeller.

Spinne...

One of the thirty-eight main fuel tanks.

Capacity 224 gallons.

Starting Engine.

Petrol Tank for Starting Engine.

650 h.p. Beardmore Diesel Engine.

...tting Device

Funnel→

...quick release of fuel in ...ergency the bottom of ...e tank may be cut open.

Knife Knife Roller

Roller Roller

...Inclined plane which ...forces knives into botton ...tank & cuts it away.

One of the five power cars.

Diagram of the method employe... warming & ventilating passenger accommodation.

Ve...

Upp.. Deck

Cable to winch for raising & lowering radiator.

Fan.

Cool air entering

Radiator... connected to Engines.

Fan Motor.

Air Inlet.

Position of radiat.. lowered in warm weather.

Mooring Arrangements & Passenger Gangway.

Bow Look out Man.

Reinforced Bow.

Gas Bag.

Ladder. Port & Starboard Winches.

Bow Winch.

Mooring Eye

Window

Hawse Pipe.

Interior Gangway running whole length of the ship.

Side Mooring Guys.

Emergency Water Ballast Bag.

Access Gangway to Mooring Mast. stowed.

Door.

Chart Table.

Chart Room. Looking down into Control Car.

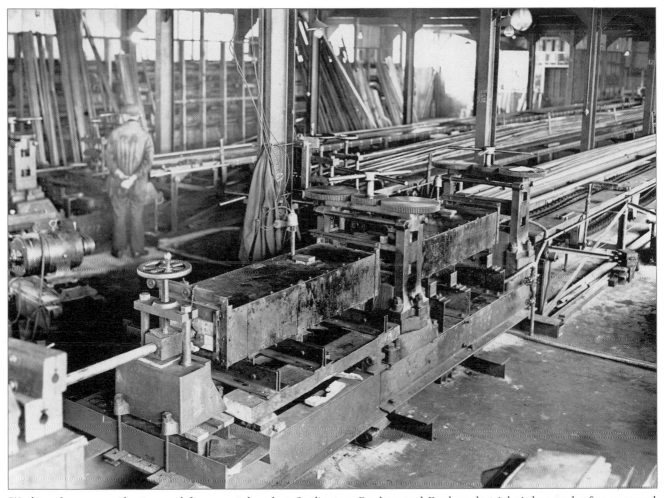

Working from a specification and figures produced at Cardington, Boulton and Paul made trial girders and, after approval from the Royal Airship Works, manufacture began in January 1927 on those parts of the airship for which the designs had been completed. This is the 70 ft long drawbench with integral tempering furnaces, invented by J.D. North for rolling and sealing the stainless steel girders for R101's mainframe at Boulton and Paul's Riverside Works in Norwich.

Girders for the main rings laid out in the Riverside Works awaiting rail shipment from Norwich to Cardington. Working to a tolerance of 1/10,000 of an inch, it is an indication of the superb workmanship of Boulton and Paul that not one piece of girderwork or tubing was rejected as being unsatisfactory.

Boulton and Paul craftsmen working on some of the duralumin girders used in the construction of the passenger accommodation. A similar girder to that on the left of the picture is now in the collection of the Airship Heritage Trust, on permanent loan from Boulton and Paul.

Above and opposite: On arrival at No.1 Shed at Cardington the pieces were laid out like a giant Meccano set. The main supporting rings of the hull – a completed one to serve as a pattern can be seen on the end wall with three more in course of construction on the floor – were assembled flat and then hoisted into position. Work on the rings began in December 1927. The third of these three photographs shows the progress of the work at the end of April, and gives a vivid idea of construction methods. By July 1928 rings 4 to 11 had been erected. Seen from the partly completed hull framework, an idea of scale can be gained from the men working at the benches on the extreme left, about halfway up.

Above and opposite: Two views of the joints which held the framework together. The assembly was greatly simplified and standardised to allow pre-fabrication of parts. There was over 30,000 feet of girder work and tubing, and literally miles of electrical and bracing wire. The frame was so strongly constructed that most of it survived the crash-landing and fire intact.

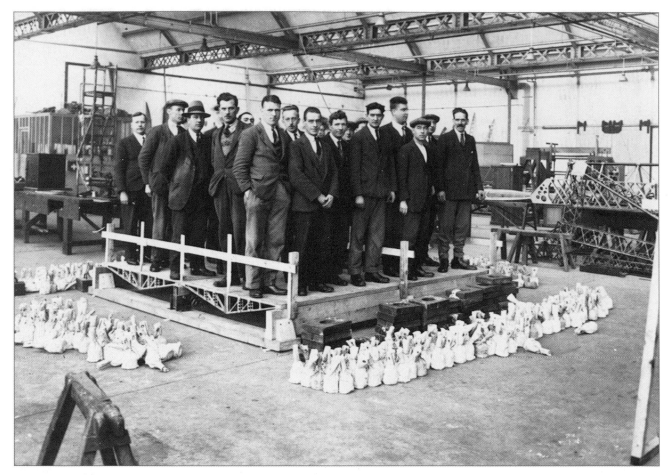

Load testing was important throughout, and here is a group of construction workers proof-loading some sample decking for the passenger accommodation.

Opposite: A workman in the partly constructed keel which ran the length of the airship, giving access to all parts. Rigid airships were laid down exactly like marine ships, and earlier ones were built 'from the keel up'. In America, where two massive rigid airships were constructed in the 1930s for the US Navy, there were even great celebrations to mark the driving home of the symbolic 'golden rivet' in the first completed hull ring.

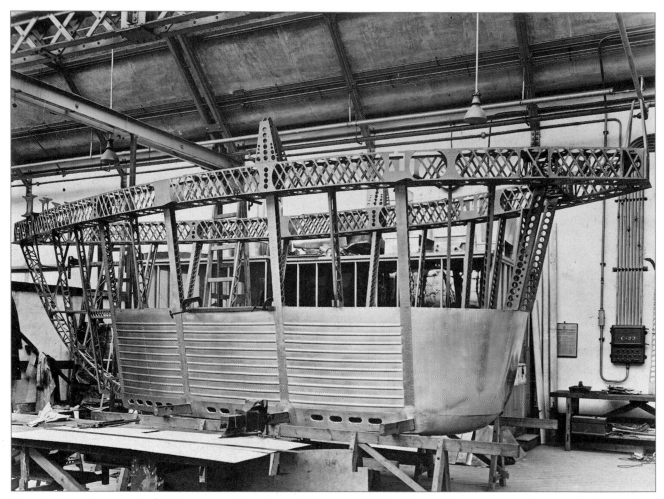

The tiny control car, only 20 ft long, was slung beneath the main hull and coupled up in August 1928. The chart room, wireless room, all the accommodation and facilities were situated within the hull itself. R101's clean lines were broken only by the little control car and the engine cars.

The bow section of R101 nearing completion and almost ready for hoisting into position. In the left foreground is the actual mooring attachment. Taken in October 1928, this photograph shows the progress of the work a year before the launch.

The huge empennage under construction on the shed floor.

Hoisting the framework of the stern out of its scaffolding, 29 November 1928.

The fins, rudders and elevators were the last part of the framework to go up. Once the structure was complete it underwent further loading and pressure trials to see if it would fail under stress. Here the entire tail section is hung with shot and sandbags to establish the load of the structure. The workmen sitting on the structure then monitored the results on loading gauges.

The testbed for Michael Rope's servo-control system, far in advance of anything seen on airships before. Driven by electric motors, the servos did away with the need for posts, pulleys and lengthy control wires, making the operation of large control surfaces much easier. Like all Rope's innovations it worked well. Other examples of his inventive mind included the wind-driven variable pitch propellers at the nose of each engine car which drove the airship's electricity generators, and the 'air log', a device that could be lowered 50 ft below the ship to record her speed accurately through electrical impulses.

The 'bridge' of R101 in the control car. With the helmsman's wheel at the front, the height (elevator) coxswain's wheel is to starboard, with the altimeter offset slightly so that he can read it with ease sideways. The instruments are basic and one, a manometer to show gas pressure, is not found in any other aircraft but an airship. Not visible in the picture are the ballast and gas controls. A clutch of speaking tubes to various parts of the ship almost masks the telegraph board for the engine cars.

The control car telegraph board, exactly like that of a marine ship, for sending directions to the five engine cars: two port, two starboard and one stern.

The linen outer cover was pre-doped to save on time and the number of men who would otherwise have had to be put up in slings to dope the cover *in situ* on the frame. Like everything else on R101, it underwent rigorous tests to see how much stress it took under load; a sample of each component was tested to destruction. Even so, problems showed up at an early stage, with some pre-doped panels tearing whilst being fixed to the frame.

The frame was covered with a number of pre-shaped fabric panels which were pulled together and then stitched to the framework as shown here. A number of 'reefing girders' between the main longitudinals were then cranked out to take up any slack in the cover, and this gave R101 her rounded, beautifully aerodynamic cross-section. The joins were then covered by tapes, glued in place.

Failure of the pre-doped outer cover at the top of the bow seems the most likely explanation for the ultimate disaster on 5 October 1930. That crucial area is seen in this view, taken during the process of stretching and stitching the linen panels of the hull covering.

The tail section nearing completion. The uncovered part where the tailplane joins the hull shows two gas bags and their attendant gas valves in place.

Opposite: The rest of the tail section, showing the tiny 'crow's nest' at the very end of the airship. This was used for meteorological observations among other things, and the Ship's Ensign flew here.

Applying the top coat of aluminium paint to the outside of the hull, and painting the international identification letter on the upper fin.

Opposite: Another view of the bows, showing the 'gills', lowered loading hatch, and the small hatches for the handling lines (open). The workmen's cradle at the mooring cone, and the onlookers below the ship give scale to her vast size.

The bow of the ship complete, with her loading hatch lowered and proudly wearing her new registration 'G-FAAW'. The black triangle halfway up the hull is a radiator for the engine car below. The holes, which admitted air for a system of 'pulsing vents' (like the gills of a fish) to keep the hull flushed (thus preventing a potentially fatal build-up of valved hydrogen, which might not otherwise escape), have yet to be cut out, and show up as a ring of bumps around the nose.

A stunning view of the finished airship filling No. 1 Shed. As in the bows, the exhaust holes of the hull-flushing system have yet to be cut out around the tail. Note the relative scale of the group of men standing to the left of the platform ladder below the left-hand engine car.

CHAPTER THREE

Inside R101

With the framework complete and the outer cover well advanced, fitting-out could begin in earnest. This is the saloon, 60 ft by 32 ft, looking across the beam of the ship with the walls, benches and electric lights in place. The headroom was 8 ft 4 in. On the far side is one of two so-called 'promenade decks'.

Aeroplanes of the 1920s were still cramped, noisy and uncomfortable, needing frequent stops to refuel and allow their passengers to rest. By contrast travellers aboard an airship, if it was big enough, could enjoy every luxury afforded by an ocean liner – saloons, dining room, promenade decks, proper private cabins, peace, quiet and comfort. An airship could theoretically stay aloft until its fuel and provisions were exhausted, so doing away with the need for frequent stops. R101 was no exception in luxury, and nothing like her was seen until Germany built the *Hindenburg* in 1935.

Those lucky enough to have been invited aboard R101 were all struck by her comfort and luxurious fittings. There was even an airtight smoking room and, ironically, one of the survivors of the disaster had been in there when the forced landing occurred. Passengers could enjoy *haute cuisine* from the all-electric galley with stewards to wait on them, and then fox-trot the night away to the accompaniment of the ship's gramophone: Paul Whiteman's *My Blue Heaven* had been a particular favourite on the R100 trip to Canada!

Opposite and above: Two more views of the passenger lounge without its ceiling, one looking for'ard with the bows in the distance, the other across the ship, clearly show the construction. Very few other pictures have survived of the ship's interior, so not much is known of her cabins or wireless room. At least one double bunk, a chair and a table thought to have been removed when the ship was lengthened have survived intact, together with sundry bits of crockery and cutlery 'removed' as souvenirs by RAW workers.

Two views of the saloon fully fitted out for the visit of 114 Members of Parliament on 23 November 1929 – including curtains, potted plants and deckchairs on the promenade decks. Flying Officer Maurice Steff had been sent to Bedford to buy tablecloths, and the ferns and flowers had been tastefully arranged by Col. Richmond's secretary. Few details have survived of the furnishings, some of which came from R36, Britain's earlier experimental passenger airship. Blue was the key colour; a royal blue carpet that ran from the entrance hatch at the bows all the way down the catwalk to the accommodation used up a lot of precious weight allowance.

R101's Chief Steward Albert Savidge, a veteran of the White Star line who left the sea for an aerial career, awaits a party of MPs to dine aboard R101 at the masthead on 23 November 1929. A flight had been planned, but weather and maintenance work prevented it. Nor was the food prepared in the ship's electric galley – it was cooked in the Royal Airship Works, brought up the mast stairs, and was practically cold by the time poor Savidge served it!

The 'promenade decks', 32 ft long, 6 ft 6 in high, had 8 ft high cellon windows let into the outer cover. A wonderful view of the passing scenery could be had – the log of one early trial flight over Norfolk recalls how passengers were able to watch foxhounds pursuing their quarry with a local hunt.

Fitting the decorative carved pillars on one of the promenade decks. Although they look substantial, the pillars were made of balsa wood.

The bow end of the lounge showing the corridor which led to the passenger cabins, and the rail of the stairs to the lower deck. Note the electric lights.

Fitting out the cabin area: a workman glues on a canvas strip to mask a join along the corridor wall. It looks cosy and private enough, but to save weight all the walls were made of canvas and the cabin doors were just single curtains.

A rigid airship is like a lot of separate balloons – gas bags, or cells – held together by an external framework. R101 was designed with sixteen gas bags, and another was added in June 1930 when it was decided that she was too heavy, and needed additional lift to be capable of carrying a realistic payload. Each gas bag was made from part of the gas-tight intestines of oxen – known as goldbeater's skin – stuck together and bonded on to canvas. Something over 100,000 oxen gave their all for R101's gas bags! Here the girls of the fabric shop are seen cleaning the intestines, a messy and smelly job.

Bonding the glued skins on to the canvas for making the gas bag.

Opposite, top: The staff, largely female, of the Fabric Shop at Cardington, 1928. They made the gas cells and the outer cover for R101.

Opposite, bottom: Glueing the individual goldbeater's skins together. Each crescent shape represents the amount of material from one ox, and there are around eighty in this picture alone.

Joining the sheets on the shed floor. Great care had to be taking in bonding the seams to ensure a gas-tight seal. A scale model of a completed gas bag for use as a pattern can be seen on a stand in the middle of the picture.

Sewing patches into the gas bags prior to fitting the gas valves, one of which can be seen on the floor in the background.

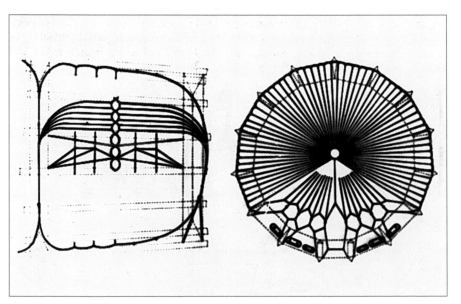

The ingenious gas bag harness invented by Michael Rope. Rather like two parachute harnesses joined end to end, the harness was designed not only to retain the bag when it was fully inflated, but also to transmit lift to the main structure of the airship. The main hull was originally intended to roll around the bags during rough weather so that they were not caused to vent gas unnecessarily. It is unlikely that Rope was to blame for the subsequent problems encountered when the bags were let out beyond their intended limit in a vain attempt to gain more lift – they snagged and tore on bolts and rivets in the frame, which meant 4,000 sharp obstacles had to be 'lagged' with canvas and tape.

Looking aft in the ship with her outer cover on and all the gas bag harnesses in place. The bags themselves have yet to be added. The blaze of light in the centre of the picture comes from the open uncompleted tail section. This view gives an idea of the immensity of the construction, with the partly completed supports for the passenger accommodation and control car right at the bottom of the picture. Also seen are some of the lozenge-shaped fuel tanks fixed to the frame each side of the passenger accommodation, which helps to explain why the final fire was fiercest at this point.

A fully inflated gas bag of 500,000 cubic feet – probably the additional bag added in the summer of 1930 – seen from the rear. Each bag took around three days to inflate with hydrogen – a tricky operation done under nets to ensure the bag inflated evenly. The riggers lend scale, as does one of the Merryweather wheeled escape ladders extensively used in the building of R101.

A partly inflated gas bag from the front. One of the main problems experienced on test flights was 'surging' of the bags back and forth, possibly because they were not held rigidly in shape by the harnesses. Although improved, this problem was never satisfactorily solved.

One of the automatic gas valves, the work of Michael Rope again, shown open. These valves were situated one on each side of each gas bag. If any gas was vented it was not allowed to settle in the hull, but was swept away by a current of air coming through the hull between the outer cover and the gas bags from a circle of holes in the bow. Pushed along by the 'pulsing vents' at ring 7 and elsewhere, it then exited through similar holes at the tail. It is possible that this arrangement caused the valves to be sucked open accidentally when air rushed past them, which could have contributed to the 'surging'. They also opened unintentionally when the ship rolled.

A closed gas valve.

Testing the valves in the annexe at Cardington.

Welding the fuel tanks. Some of these were designed to be jettisoned complete through the outer cover as ballast in an emergency.

Making the engine cars. These were very cramped when occupied by a main engine, an auxiliary starter petrol engine, its fuel tank, and one or two engineers.

Opposite: All fuel tanks were capable of jettisoning their fuel if necessary; some tanks were jettisoned complete, while others were designed with a bizarre 'tin-opener' arrangement that cut off the base of the tank, spilling the contents. Here one of the latter is tested. R101 used heavy diesel oil for fuel, as it was felt that a lot of petrol would be too dangerously combustible in the heat of Egypt and India where she was scheduled to travel.

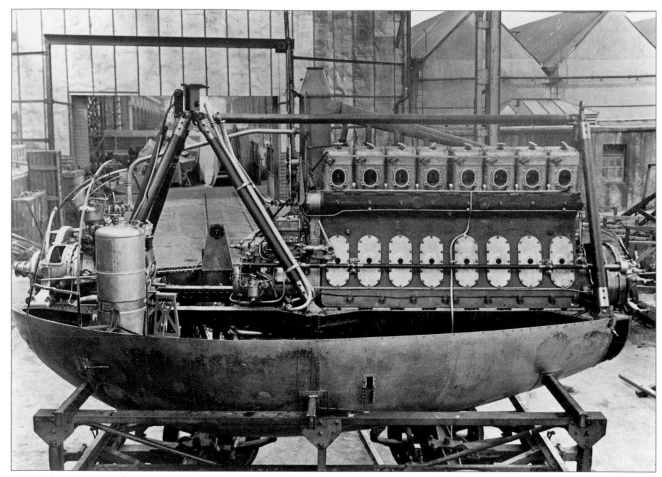

A 525 h.p. Beardmore Tornado diesel engine (port side) installed in the bottom half of the engine car. Originally developed for railway locomotives in Canada the engines, of which R101 had five, were seriously overweight for the airship. An intended lighter replacement (the Typhoon) was not ready in time. The first of the Tornados arrived for gantry tests at Cardington in the autumn of 1928.

Starboard side of the same engine. The stench of fuel and the noise in the 'power eggs' when the engines were running can only be imagined.

Front end of a partly uncovered engine car. Each car had one of Michael Rope's wind-driven generators, whose propeller was fixed to the little hub seen at the front of the engine. All together they provided R101's electrical power.

The dismantled hub in this rear view of the engine car exposes the intricate gearing necessary for the variable-pitch and reversible propellers. Unfortunately, these propellers failed owing to the vibration from the vast 'straight-eight' engines and had to be replaced with wooden ones, which initially could not be run in reverse.

A steel propeller in place on Cardington's engine test rig in October 1928. The cable running from the propeller boss was secured to a point some 50 ft further back on the hull framework and was supposed to take some of the strain as the engine 'pushed' the airship forward.

The highly advanced, variable-pitch reversible steel propellers for R101 were made by Metal Propellers Ltd of Croydon. Here the 16 ft diameter rear propeller, said to be the largest metal propeller constructed up to that date, is tested on a jig in their workshop.

The rear engine car and the other four 'outrigger' engine cars were finally installed on the airship between July and September 1929.

CHAPTER FOUR

Infrastructure
for the Imperial Airship Route

While the airship herself had been in the planning stages and was being built, the route that she was to fly, to India initially, had been surveyed, and all the stations at which she might stop *en route* were being prepared. No. 2 Shed from Pulham had been brought to Cardington to house R100, and No. 1 Shed (for R101) had been upgraded and extended. Then, in 1924, the Cleveland Bridge and Engineering Co. began construction on this 230 ft high mast at Cardington.

Another view of the mast under construction. Here part of the mooring head machinery is about to be hoisted up the central stairwell that will eventually accommodate a lift.

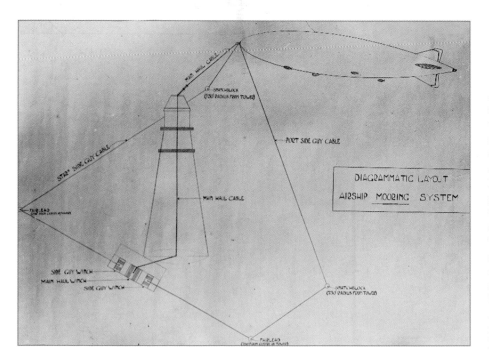

A good diagrammatic layout showing how R101 was moored to her high mast. In this system, devised and perfected by Commander E.A.D. Masterman and Major Scott at Pulham in Norfolk, the airship dropped two guys, to port and starboard, and the main haul cable was dropped at some distance to the mast. These cables were led through snatchblocks (anchored pulleys) on the airfield, and coupled to another set of cables which had been run out from the mast itself. All three steam winches in the mast building then combined to haul the airship on to the mast.

The extendable arm which received the nose cup of the airship at full stretch during the tests of the mast head equipment.

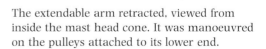

The extendable arm retracted, viewed from inside the mast head cone. It was manoeuvred on the pulleys attached to its lower end.

The shape of things to come: the mast head equipment in use with R101 attached and the extending arm retracted: it only emerged to receive the airship when she was coming on to the mast.

Once the mast with all its steam-winching gear (by Babcock and Wilcox, primarily famous for marine steam engines and steam rollers) had been completed, it was tested for loading by means of a stationary steam winch firmly anchored in the middle of the airfield. Here a technician, with a nice disregard of safety harnesses, checks loading gauges at the top of the mast.

Identical masts were built at Ismailia in Egypt (seen here) and Karachi.

The mast and hydrogen plant (extreme right of picture) at Ismailia in Egypt, the first expected major stop for R101. The Ismailia site cost over £93,000 to construct. An intermediate mast had been planned for Malta as, owing to the prevalent political situation, Italy could not be overflown; but it was not built.

A view of the gasometers at Ismailia, capable of holding sufficient hydrogen for R101, some five-and-a-half million cubic feet in all.

The shed erected at Drigh Road, Karachi (now the International Airport), was the largest building in the British Empire at the time of its construction in the mid-1920s. The scale can be gauged from the standard RAF hutments clustered around it. The shed survived into the days of India's independence, when it was pulled down and used to build and repair bridges on the Indian Railways.

The mast at Karachi was to have incorporated splendid accommodation around its base in the Anglo-Indian style of architecture. Here it is in the early stages of construction. A similar mast at St Hubert Airport, Montreal, was built in a 'Regency' style by the Canadian Government and used by R100 on her Canada flight in 1930. Had the R101 made it to Karachi, the next stage was to have been masts, sheds and facilities in Australia, the ultimate destination of the Imperial Airship Service.

An interesting aerial view of the site at Karachi, with long shadows revealing the great shed and gas plant on the right, the mast in the middle, and conventional aeroplane hangars on the left. The whole Karachi site cost nearly £250,000 to develop, a huge sum in the Depression years. It was never used by an airship.

CHAPTER FIVE

Service Life

The day that the Royal Airship Works had been awaiting for five years. At 0545 hrs on Saturday 12 October 1929, with the help of 200 constructors from the RAW, 150 airmen from RAF Halton and 50 unemployed persons recruited from Bedford Labour Exchange, R101 was brought out of her shed to a great cheer from a considerable crowd of townspeople lining the Bedford to Shefford road. It is estimated that 4 tons of dust blew off her back as she emerged into the light dawn breeze. The tiny black dot breaking the line of the hull above the bows is Noel 'Grabby' Atherstone, First Officer, supervising the mooring ropes.

Following her 'roll-out' R101 moved crabwise across the airfield at Cardington as dawn broke on 12 October. It took an hour and fifty minutes to get her the half mile from the shed into a position where she could be winched on to the

mooring mast. Large airships were generally handled at dawn or late evening when calmer weather and light winds were more likely.

Once in the lee of the mast she was coupled to the mooring wires and allowed to rise to the height of the tower. When this picture was taken at around 0730 hrs she was about 200 ft up and had hit an inversion, a layer of warm air above the cold air at airfield level, which reduced her buoyancy. Two tons of water had to be discharged.

A spectacular view taken from the port bow hatch of R101 showing the descent to the mast. The port guy dominates the foreground, and the main haul cable leads from the bow to the masthead. The cloud of steam enveloping the engine house suggests that the winches are running full ahead. The masthead arm is fully extended to receive the nose cup.

Height of Mast 210 ft
Entrance of Airship on Mooring Mast.
Becomes a covered passage for passengers, who
are taken to Mast-head by lift

Safely down, with her nose cup locked home and the mast's extendable arm retracted, R101 rides at the mast. The entrance hatch is lowered, and a crewman takes a bow in the opening. This was the only way in and out of the airship, so canvas screens were normally rigged each side of the entrance to hide the 230 ft drop from faint-hearted passengers.

Photographed from the mast, Engineer M.F. Littlekitt demonstrates that the way in and out of the engine cars is even more perilous than using the bow hatch!

Even in the open the sheer size of R101 was overwhelming. The little DH60 Gypsy Moth which appears to be directly over the airship was 24 ft long with a wingspan of 30 ft, and that tiny bump of a control car beneath R101 was 20 ft long: the resulting perspective shows that the Moth is actually much nearer to the photographer than the airship is! A 2 mile air exclusion zone operated around Cardington when either R100 or R101 was moored on the mast.

Left and overleaf: These two photographs, taken from the original glass plates, show the grace and elegance of the newly launched airship's lines.

An unusual ventral view of the new ship on the mast, showing the louvred caps over the 'pulsing vents' on her flanks, and a trick of the light giving a strange, crinkly effect to her cellon saloon windows.

Another optical illusion apparently showing the airship dwarfing No. 2 Shed, which is actually over half a mile distant from the mast.

On Monday 14 October, R101 slipped the mast at 1117 hrs in warm sunny weather with a light breeze blowing, circled Bedford, and headed for London, passing over Buckingham Palace, Westminster, St Paul's and the City, returning five hours later. In a view shared by R101's officers, *The Times* remarked: 'A more perfect operation could not be desired – a happy augury for the future.'

A happy group of riggers and engineers at the base of the mast after the maiden flight. Joe Binks is arrowed, with Alf Cook (who bears an uncanny resemblance to Charlie Chaplin) standing next to him: both were survivors at Allonne.

A rural view of R101 riding to the Cardington mast; occasionally she was let up on her line above mast height, 'like a great silver salmon played on a line'. She left an indelible impression on everyone who saw her. The shire horses and timber drug belonged to a farmer from Cople.

Four days later R101 climbs away for an extended test flight over the West Midlands. Despite overcast rainy conditions she performed well, but it was already apparent that she was considerably overweight.

On 1 November, R101 flew 'home' to Norwich to salute the workers at Boulton and Paul. Taken from the roof of the old Municipal Buildings, the quality of the photograph is far from perfect, but it is the only known picture of R101 above the city of her birth: she appears to be suspended between the cathedral and the castle on her run-in to the Riverside Works. Earlier in the day she had flown round the North Norfolk coast from King's Lynn, passing low over Sandringham House where Their Majesties, King George V and Queen Mary, waved to her. Sir Samuel Hoare was on board, and was treated to an aerial view of his home near Cromer. R101 then returned to Bedford via Thetford, Newmarket and Cambridge.

R101 was besieged by visitors in the next few weeks, and here is one such group on the gallery of the mast. On 23 November 1929 114 MPs had lunch on R101, but had to climb 170 ft up the mast's open staircase because the lift was out of action. Luckily the weather was too bad to take them for a flight as planned, because the ship was grossly overloaded with 148 people on board. However, the combination of 45 m.p.h. winds and the running-up of the engines to provide heating caused amusement amongst the crew because '. . . some of the party got drunk and were convinced they had been taken for a longish flight . . .'!

Passengers boarding R101 for a test flight. The bow 'gill' holes are shown to advantage, and the crewman in the starboard bow hatch keeps an eye on some of the flexible pipes used for gassing, fuelling and watering the airship.

Another visitor in 1929 was HRH the Prince of Wales (later Edward VIII).

Sleeping giants. In April 1930 the 'rival' ship, R100, was lodged in No. 2 Shed at Cardington (on the right) in readiness for her flight to Canada on 25 July, giving an unknown photographer this remarkable view with R101 in the depths of No. 1 Shed.

R100 on the Cardington mast following her return from Montreal, 16 August 1930. The popular press liked to inflame rivalries between the ships they had styled the 'Socialist' R101 and the 'Capitalist' R100. Controversy has reigned ever since, and those who prefer to remain untroubled by the huge amount of indisputable evidence to the contrary *still* condemn R101 as 'bad', and applaud R100 as 'good'. Much of the blame for this attitude rests with R100's heavily biased Chief Calculator N.S. Norway – author Nevil Shute – who gave vent to his prejudices in his book *Sliderule*. The gullible have accepted the Shute version as gospel ever since, but the true story is far more interesting.

Near-panic ensued when the initial test flights showed R101 was too heavy for her projected flight to India. In late July 1930 she was taken back to No. 1 Shed for two months, split in half and given an additional bay and gas bag, bringing her total length from 732 to 777 ft. It did not help disposable lift much either – in addition to the airship's weight of 117 tons, the disposable lift was only 42 tons, of which 18 tons was taken up by the crew, ballast, movable equipment, etc., leaving only 24 tons for fuel, oil and her payload. The resultant payload, around 4 tons, was totally inadequate.

Another view taken when R101 was lengthened. One interesting feature revealed is the two pairs of water ballast bags, well described by German airshipmen as 'trousers'!

A beautiful picture of the lengthened R101 riding to the Cardington mast in the sunshine of early October 1930. Some said that by being 'stretched', her lines had been spoiled and '. . . if it doesn't look right, it won't fly right'. Note the use of large cricket pitch rollers, slung below the hull, to help keep the ship steady at the mast. If the wind changed and the airship weathercocked, the rollers would go with her.

There is no known photograph which shows all the crew of R101 together at one time, but here are some of the main personalities gathered below the ship in No. 1 Shed. In the front row are the coxswains 'Mush' Oughton (extreme left), who had flown the ship at the RAF Pageant at Hendon in June, and 'Tich' Mason (fifth from left). In the centre of the second row 'Bird' Irwin sits with his cap at a jaunty angle, and to his left (immediately behind Mason) the hunched, almost weary figure of Major Scott, his face hidden by his cap. Next to Scott is 'Grabby'

Atherstone, then Maurice Steff and Chief Engineer Bill Gent. On Irwin's right, the Navigator Ernest Johnston, Chief Coxswain 'Sky' Hunt and, quite literally Hunt's right-hand man, Wally Potter. On the extreme left stands Engineer Burton, whose personal effects, retrieved from his body at Allonne, are now in the AHT Collection. On the third row, behind Wally Potter stands Joe Binks, a survivor. Arthur Bell, another engineer who survived, is second from the right in the back row.

Flt. Lt. Carmichael 'Bird' Irwin (1894–1930), pictured at tea aboard R36, was the Commander of R101. A tall, sensitive Irishman, he had flown non-rigid airships in Home Waters and the Eastern Mediterranean in the Great War, and had commanded R33 and R36 from 1920. When R33 was laid up he was posted as Commandant of the Balloon School at Larkhill, but was recalled to take command of R101. He was a fine middle-distance runner, a member of the British Olympic team at Antwerp in 1920, and a singularly talented airship pilot. He could always be relied on to make a good landing even in foul weather, but for some reason he was often over-ridden by Major Scott at key moments, sometimes with calamitous results.

CHAPTER SIX

More Personalities

That most pivotal and controversial figure of British airship history, Major Scott, in the control car of R101. All agree that he had a touch of genius about him, and his ability to solve seemingly insoluble problems overnight in his sleep became legendary. But there was an impetuous side to his nature which led to the nickname of 'Press-on' Scott, and he sometimes had trouble in communicating his intentions to other members of his crew. This was a flaw which, in the heat of the moment, may have contributed to ending the service careers of R36, when she ran on to the Pulham mast in 1921, and R33, when she hit the shed doors at Pulham four years later. By 1929 his original force, drive and (so some critics claimed) his judgement had diminished somewhat. Photographic evidence suggests he wasn't quite the man he had been. This may have had serious implications for R101 – Scott's 'press-on' attitude and a certain willingness to please the crowds probably helped to seal her fate. But his reputation meant that his position in the programme was unchallenged, and 'Scottie' was always popular with his crews, for whom he showed an almost fatherly affection at times. Although his role on board R101 was supposed to be that of 'admiral' to Irwin's 'captain', it did not always appear that way in practice.

Flying Officer Maurice Steff (1896–1930), the Second Officer, with Noel Grabowsky Atherstone, Atherstone's dog Tim, 'Bird' Irwin, and Chief Designer Vincent Richmond standing in No. 1 Shed with R101 behind them. Despite his relative inexperience with airships, it is likely that Steff was in command when R101 took her death plunge, Irwin and Atherstone having just gone off watch at 0200 hrs, although Michael Rope and 'Sky' Hunt were known to have been on hand at the time. Atherstone's widow knew instinctively that her husband was dead when Tim gave an unearthly howl at the exact moment R101 was lost. Irwin's widow also knew the instant that 'Bird' had died; as she later explained, they both shared Celtic presentiment: 'we both knew he wasn't coming back'.

Noel Grabowsky Atherstone (1894–1930), First
Officer of R101, he had Polish ancestry and was
born in St Petersburg. He had qualified as an
airship pilot with the RNAS in 1917. Previously
just Grabowsky, he adopted his wife's name of
Atherstone in 1919, but was always known as
'Grabby'. Incredibly, he seems to have a cigarette
in his hand – something that was strictly
forbidden in the vicinity of the hydrogen-filled
airship. Standing behind Atherstone is T.S.D.
Collins of the Cardington Design Staff who was
present on all the test flights, and already had the
designs of R102 and R103 well advanced by the
time that the loss of R101 spelt the end of the
airship programme.

Maurice Giblett (1894–1930), Chief
Meteorological Officer at Cardington. One of the
true pioneers who laid the foundations of the
science of aviation meteorology, he had been
involved with lighter-than-air flight since the
1920s when he took part in the international
Gordon Bennett Balloon Races.

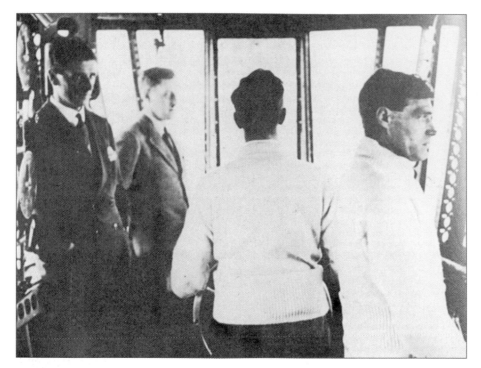

A very rare in-flight picture of Irwin, Atherstone, Coxswain Wally Potter and Chief Coxswain George 'Sky' Hunt (1889–1930) in the control car of R101. Hunt, who had been in the Guard of Honour at the funeral of aviation pioneer 'Colonel' S.F. Cody in 1912, could trace his airship involvement back to 1914, and was undoubtedly the most knowledgeable and capable airship NCO in the country. It is said that, in true NCO style, he could swear continuously for ten minutes without repeating himself. He and Potter were inseparable friends, and legend has it that Hunt escaped from the wreckage of R101, only to go back into the inferno to rescue Potter. Both were killed.

Thomas Megginson (1912–30) was the galley boy of R101 and her youngest victim at just eighteen years old. Known as 'Jim' on account of his sunny disposition, the Yorkshire lad from Cawood had been chosen for the job from more than 500 applicants, and had already flown to Canada with R100 despite being under age at seventeen. He considered that in his position he would be 'made for life'. His body could not be identified after the fire, and when his family came to Cardington for the mass burial his father handed a wreath to a bearer with the heart-broken words: 'Put this on one o' the longer coffins . . . he were a tall lad.'

R101's resident cook, J.F. Meegan, at the masthead in a stiff breeze with the bows of R101 filling the skyline beyond the parapet. He was not on the last flight – Eric Graham was chosen, and died as a result. Another cook had been suspended pending an inquiry over his demands for 'danger money' to work on R101.

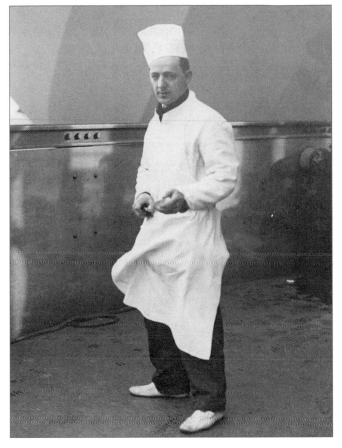

Chef Meegan being supervised in his all-electric galley by Chief Steward Albert Savidge. Popular and dependable, Savidge was also a talented artist who amused his crew mates by drawing cartoons for them.

Sam Church, a rigger who was sent into the bow of R101 to release water ballast immediately prior to her forced landing. Although badly injured, he survived and was able to give valuable information which was used at the subsequent Court of Inquiry. His parents and fiancée set out for Beauvais immediately on hearing news of the disaster, but Sam died of his injuries on 8 October, only a few hours before they reached his bedside. He was twenty-six.

India Flight –
Appointment with Fate

The clouds lower on 4 October as R101, looking decidedly weather-worn, rides on the mast awaiting her passengers and crew.

The year 1930 was remarkable for aviation. Amy Johnson flew solo from England to Australia in her tiny DH60 Gypsy Moth *Jason*. Germany's *Graf Zeppelin* was trailblazing non-stop routes everywhere and about to circumnavigate the globe. The 'rival' R100 flew the north Atlantic to Canada and back to great acclaim. America was planning her huge aeroplane-carrying airships, and it was obvious that for global communications airships would be unbeaten in the foreseeable future. It was the year of the Imperial Conference in Delhi, and since Lord Thomson had prepared a paper about communications within the Empire what better way to prove the point than by arriving in India by airship? What an impact *that* would make, especially as a new Viceroy of India would be named at the Conference – a post for which Thomson was ambitious. He made it known that R101 would be ready to fly to Karachi at the beginning of October, almost at any cost. The ship was, he said, 'Safe as houses – except for the millionth chance'.

The final trials were rushed through, (not altogether satisfactorily) and there was still trouble with the state of the pre-doped outer cover when the appointed departure day came. There was disquiet in the CAA about the granting of a Certificate of Airworthiness. Saturday 4 October 1930 was cold, wet, and windy. The crew were far from optimistic: they knew R101 was overloaded – Thomson took a huge amount of luggage, including a valuable Persian carpet for use at a banquet to be held at Ismailia *en route* – and the weather was hardly conducive to that 'happy augury for the future' which *The Times* had spoken about. There were tales of riotous sprees by the airshipmen in the Bell public house at Cotton End, and the teenage son of an employee there alleged that Major Scott spent a lot of late nights drinking with Colmore and Richmond until time was called. If this is true, it may be that many of the decisions to modify the structure of R101 were made at the Bell without the benefit of consultation or sound advice from the self-effacing teetotaller, Michael Rope. On the afternoon of 4 October, Coxswain 'Sky' Hunt had parted from his fourteen-year-old son Albert with the words: 'Look after your Mother, boy: this old rag-bag won't make it', and several of the crew forbade their families and loved ones to see the ship off, preferring that they should remember them quietly in their own homes. It is reasonable to assume that morale was at an all-time low when His Majesty's Airship R101 lurched away from the mast that evening, plunged alarmingly, dropped 2 tons of water ballast, and lumbered away into the gloom, the wet and the rising wind.

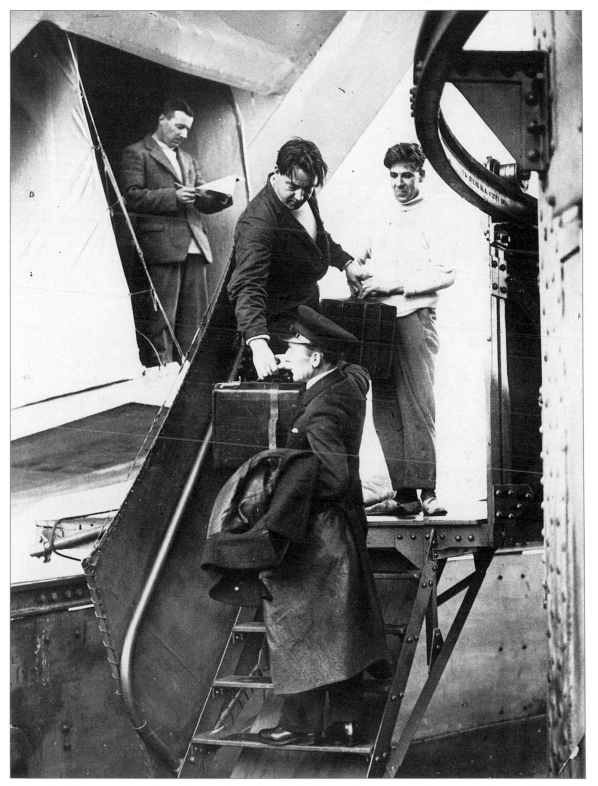

Personal effects coming on board in readiness for the flight to India on 4 October 1930. Flying Officer Steff checks them off at the bow hatch. Everything had to be carefully weighed, even to the extent of biscuits being removed from their tins to make the load lighter.

The Director of Civil Flying, Sir Sefton Brancker, no doubt joking about the incongruity of solar topees on such a foul evening, with some of the crew of R101 before they ascended the mast for the last time on 4 October 1930. That famous rimless monocle was the key to the identification of Brancker's remains after the fire, and it is sobering to reflect that less than ten hours after the photograph was taken only one person pictured here was still alive – Engineer Arthur Bell (second left) escaped from the aft engine car.

One of the last known pictures to have been taken of R101, at around 1830 hrs on Saturday 4 October 1930. The engines are running up, the saloon lights are lit, and she swings gently at the mast in gloomy drizzle. Major Scott had received a weather report informing him that the bad weather front would pass in seven hours and then R101 would have clear weather and a following wind all the way to Egypt. But no; Lord Thomson was anxious to get to India for the conference, the journalists and the film cameras were there, and so was a huge crowd to cheer them off. An eyewitness reported that Scott 'screwed up the report and threw it on the shed floor with the words "Let's press on"', but the veracity of that account cannot now be proved.

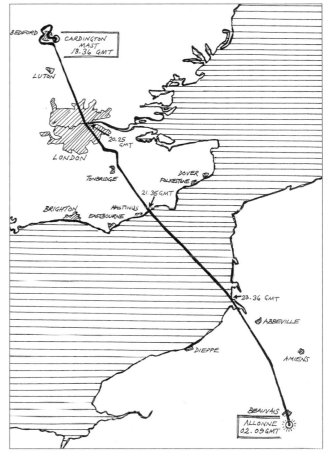

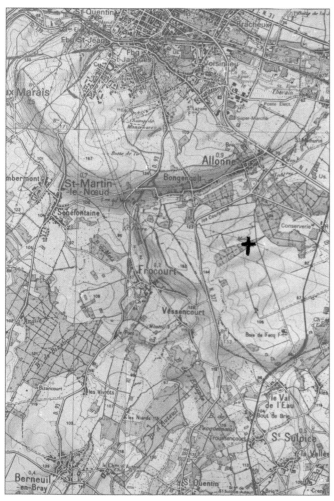

The course taken by R101 that fateful evening, and a close-up of the Bois du Coutumes area near Allonnes where the airship was destroyed. The actual point of impact is marked with a cross.

Having circled Bedford, R101 was already fighting a battle against a rising wind. With little progress in the first half hour, an altitude of only 600 ft, and a ground speed of 35 mph, it is certain that a possible return to Cardington was discussed. But they pressed on in spite of No. 5 engine being shut down over London, and crossed the coast at Haddocks Gap near Hastings three hours after departure. Two hours later the errant engine was started again and they crossed the French coast. In the teeth of the storm their speed dropped to 22 mph and the airship lost more height in low-level turbulence. She had drifted 15 miles off course, and ahead lay the Beauvais Ridge, notorious for strange wind patterns and vicious down-draughts.

Two survivors recalled later that they had looked out of their engine car to see the pinnacles of a great church loom out of the darkness on a level with them – R101 had almost hit Beauvais Cathedral. She came over the Beauvais Ridge at Bois du Coutumes, still losing height. As the morning watch under the relatively inexperienced Maurice Steff grasped the true extent of the situation, Rigger Church was sent forward to release ballast, and fuel was jettisoned – right underneath where the airship would come to rest. She dipped once, straightened, then dipped again. A gentle impact followed, and at 0208 hrs Coxswain Hunt was heard going through the ship to warn the crew: 'We're down, lads'. Then suddenly came the explosion and fire. Eight men fought their way out of the wreckage only to find that they could not breathe because the burning hydrogen had consumed all the oxygen in the area. Two survivors later died in hospital and, although help was very quick in coming from Beauvais, nothing could be done for the forty-eight passengers and crew who had been unable to escape. The fire was so fierce that, although all the bodies were recovered from the wreckage, only five victims could be positively identified at Allonne; another twenty-one were identified from dental records or possessions back in London. Among those who were never identified was Christopher Birdwood Thomson.

The gaunt skeleton of R101 lying with her nose in the copse at the Bois du Coutumes. The following pictures show the wreckage later on the morning of 5 October.

The mooring winches thrown forward of the nose by the impact. The nose cup itself may be seen bottom left.

Above and opposite, bottom: Two pictures which show that the framework of the empennage remained fairly intact after the fabric had burnt away.

French firemen, attempting to extricate bodies from the wreckage, duck as some of the girders give way.

An engine car, inverted, still smoulders.

The Ship's Ensign, flown from the crow's nest at the tail of R101, miraculously survived the fire and was quickly recovered. It is now in the parish church at Cardington

The corpses were carefully laid on the margin of the wood, together with any effects found on or close to each body to assist identification. Most of the victims were burned beyond recognition. Here, with the skeleton of R101 behind them, a fireman, soldier and policeman gently place another rough coffin on a cart bound for the makeshift mortuary in the concert room of Beauvais Town Hall.

The gale continued into 6 October, causing a young French boy to wrap his jacket about him (lower left) as the first coffin is carried into the Town Hall.

The Mayor of Allonne, M. Felix Ballon, together with members of the town Fire Brigade who, in addition to the harrowing task of extricating the remains of the victims from the wreckage, kept a constant vigil over the coffins at the Town Hall. The strain of long hours and horrific sights shows all too clearly on their faces.

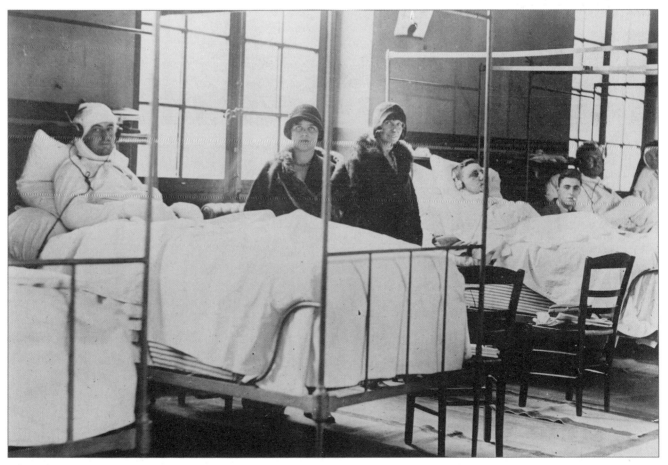

A family visit to cheer the survivors. In the nearest bed is wireless operator/electrician Arthur Disley; next to him is Alf Cook, who was on duty in the mid-port engine car. Cook was severely burned during his escape; despite this, he went on to a distinguished career in aeronautics and became the longest-lived of all the R101 survivors, dying in 1998 at the grand age of ninety-one. Beauvais hospital was primitive, built as a barracks for Napoleonic troops. It was in the care of a Nursing Order of Sisters, one of whom appears on the right of this picture. Two of the survivors, Sam Church and Walter Radcliffe, died of their injuries in the hospital.

Eighteen of twenty-four wagons, each bearing two of the forty-eight victims of the disaster in coffins draped with the Union flag, are lined up in Beauvais before the first funeral procession. A detachment of the army, an army band and the local fire brigade parade before the wagons.

The dignitaries muster. With them are three of the survivors well enough to walk in the cortège. Harry Leech, the Foreman Engineer who had been enjoying a cigarette in R101's airtight smoking room and kicked his way out when she exploded, has his head bandaged and covers his burned hands with a mackintosh; next to him is Arthur 'Ginger' Bell and then Joe Binks. These last two had been in the aft engine car and escaped when a ballast tank above them burst and doused some of the flames.

124

Part of the funeral procession in the centre of Beauvais. In addition to the army, mounted gendarmes and the fire brigade, there is a detachment of the exotic and slightly sinister-looking Spahi Cavalry. In the background come the artillery wagons bearing the dead. The obsequies rendered by the French authorities and townspeople were deep, dignified and heartfelt, ranging from tiny posies of wild flowers and lighted candles laid alongside the corpses in the wood to this solemn civic ceremonial.

Harry Leech walks between Joe Binks (left) and Arthur Bell (right) in the funeral cortège. Another engineer who had been on duty, Vic Savory, also survived, almost unscathed.

Even before the victims and survivors had started their homeward journey, air accident investigators began to sift through the wreckage of the great ship. Here the barely recognisable remains of the rear engine car come under close scrutiny.

On Tuesday 7 October the victims were taken to Boulogne and brought back across the Channel aboard the destroyer HMS *Tempest*.

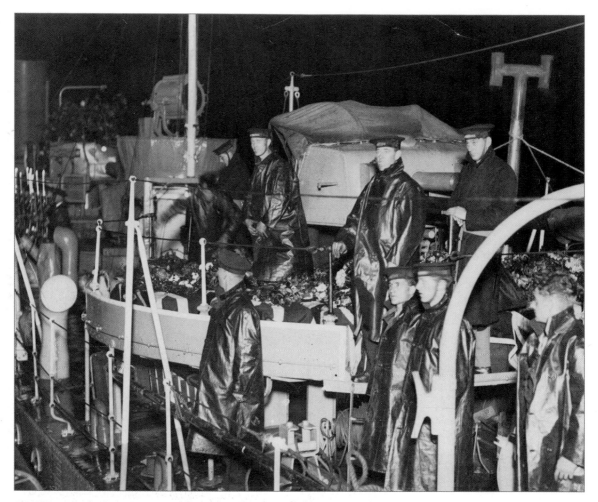

HMS *Tempest* docks at Dover in familiar conditions – darkness and driving rain.

London's Victoria station was cleared, and a special train bearing the victims from Dover, headed by an engine with a wreath fixed to its smokebox, arrived there on the stroke of midnight. Despite the late hour a huge crowd gathered outside the concourse. In their midst the first RAF tender leaves the station.

One of the twenty-four RAF tenders that took the dead to Westminster mortuary departs from Victoria station in the small hours of 8 October. Forensic experts at the mortuary managed to identify a further twenty-one of the victims from personal effects or dental records.

The victims lay in state in Westminster Hall on Friday 10 October, where thousands of people filed past to pay their last respects. From eight in the morning until half an hour after midnight they came, having queued quietly past Big Ben, right down the Embankment to Cleopatra's Needle.

On Saturday the dead of R101 were taken on twenty-four artillery carriages through the heart of London to Euston station. Here the cortège passes the Cenotaph in Whitehall.

Opposite: At noon that same day a memorial service was held in St Paul's Cathedral, with that emotive scorched ensign from the tail of R101 draped over the altar. Simultaneously, in Westminster Cathedral, a requiem mass was celebrated by Fr Harry Rope, brother of R101's Michael Rope. In this atmospheric photograph, Fr Rope stands at the altar while Cardinal Bourne kneels in the centre of the sanctuary, at the bottom of the altar steps.

A special train, double-headed by the locomotives *Arabic* and *Persia*, took the victims on the last stage to Bedford. *Arabic* (an ex-LNWR Prince of Wales class 4–6–0 of 1911) bore this floral tribute in red, white and blue, given by the staff of the London Midland and Scottish Railway.

The train drew into St John's station at Bedford at 1345 precisely, where the coffins were transferred to the twenty-four waiting RAF tenders, all resplendent with fresh grey paint and white pipe-clayed tyres.

The whole route from Bedford station to Cardington church, around 2 miles, was lined by crowds, several deep. In a solid unbroken procession, the first tender reached Cardington before the last had left the railway station.

Some of the crowds lining the Cardington road.

Dr Hugo Eckener led a little group of mourners from the Zeppelin Company. He cut an imposing figure, gloves in one hand, with Luftschiffskapitän Hans von Schiller alongside him.

Many of the dead had belonged to the Royal Antediluvian Order of Buffaloes (a Friendly Society), and their fellow Royal Airship Works 'Buffs' brought floral tributes and mustered in front of the R101's empty No. 1 Shed before setting out for Cardington cemetery.

That afternoon, in the country churchyard at Cardington within sight of the sheds and the empty mooring mast they had left exactly one week before, the forty-eight dead of R101 were laid to rest in a single mass grave. The Senior Chaplain to the RAF, the Vicar of Cardington, the Anglican Bishop of St Alban's, his Roman Catholic counterpart with acolytes and incense, and two Nonconformist ministers shared the service. It took over half an hour to lay the dead in their common grave. Dusk was falling by the time of the final RAF flypast; then 'Reveille' was sounded, and a muffled peal of bells rang from Cardington church. R101's passengers and crew were home again, one week to the hour since their ship had cast off from that mast across the fields, which was growing dimmer in the autumn evening mist.

A sea of floral tributes at the grave, including representations of the RAF cockade, a propeller, and the airship herself. The tribute from the staff of the Royal Airship Works can be seen lower left.

By October 1931 a beautiful memorial tomb inscribed with the names of the dead had been raised over the mass grave in Cardington cemetery. Although the appellation is not strictly accurate, it is always referred to as the Cenotaph.

Aftermath

The survivors were soon repatriated from Beauvais hospital, and the authorities continued sifting through the wreckage. A Court of Inquiry was convened and its findings have been the subject of heated debate ever since. It seems most likely that the disaster was caused by the failure of the outer cover and rapid deflation of the forward gas bags, which caused the nose to dip. This, coupled with the effects of a strong down-draught over the Beauvais Ridge, made the result inevitable. Even so, the wreckage showed that the impact was quite gentle, rather more of a forced landing than a crash, and the framework survived mostly intact. The fire, fiercest in the area of the passenger accommodation where much of the fuel was stored, probably began as the hot engines made contact with a lethal hydrogen/air mixture from ruptured gas bags, although one alternative view is that magnesium flares stored in the control car were ignited by water from a fractured pipe. Whatever the cause, no-one had any enthusiasm for big airships now, and the Royal Airship Works closed, dealing Bedford another massive blow in redundancies. Over the next four years a series of disasters caused the Americans to abandon their giant airship programme, and the loss of Germany's *Hindenburg* in May 1937 was the last straw.

With the loss of the Secretary of State for Air, the Director of Civil Aviation, and so many of the brightest stars of Britain's airship technicians and crewmen, it was inevitable that the Imperial Airship Programme would founder quickly. It seemed that all enthusiasm for airships had gone from Britain, swept away on the tide of a national tragedy. Development work on R102 and R103 stopped at once. R100 languished in Cardington's No. 2 Shed until January 1931, when she was broken up and her remains flattened by a steam roller: the ship that had cost almost £400,000 to build was now sold for scrap – and realised a mere £450. The near-worthless carcass of R101 lay where it had fallen until well into 1931, the haunt of air accident investigators and curious day-trippers. Finally, scrap contractors from Sheffield, specialists in stainless steel, went out to Allonne and retrieved what they could.

The Cardington mast was pulled down in 1941 to help the wartime drive for scrap metal, but the winch house remains, as does the R101 Memorial Tomb, that scorched RAF Ensign, and the two huge sheds dominating the Bedford skyline. Another impressive cenotaph honouring the dead of R101 still stands by the main autoroute south at Allonne, built by French generosity and unveiled in October 1933. The Airship Heritage Trust, a 'spiritual successor' to the Royal Airship Works, struggles to preserve photographs, pictures, artefacts and other memorabilia of those glory days of the late '20s, despite having had to leave their old home at Cardington when the RAF closed the station in April 2000. Their dedication, and that of a growing band of enthusiasts around the world, ensures that R101 and the brave men who died with her in pursuit of their fantastic dream will never be forgotten.

R100 being dismantled at Cardington in January 1931. Sold for scrap at a mere £400, her fabric was cut up and given away as prizes in a children's magazine competition. The 'imperial dream' had died with R101, and the scrapping of R100 brought a glorious enterprise to an ignominious end.

Final Specification of HMA R101, 4 October 1930

Design and Construction:	Royal Airship Works, Cardington
Sub-Contractors (framework):	Boulton and Paul Aircraft, Norwich
Length:	777 ft (originally 732 ft)
Diameter:	132 ft
Volume (cubic feet):	5,500,000 (originally (5,000,000)
Power plants:	Five 525 h.p. Beardmore 'Tornado' diesels
Gross tonnage (fully laden):	159 tons
Disposable lift (including fuel, crew, etc.):	42 tons
Practical payload:	4.5 tons
Maximum speed:	62 mph (five engines at 3,250 bhp)
Long-range cruising speed:	50 mph (five engines at 1,800 bhp)
Average number of crew:	40
Number of flights:	12
Total flying time:	127 hours 20 minutes (12 flights in 16 days)
Total hours on mooring mast:	1,039 hours 53 minutes during 43 days
Total hours out of shed:	1,167 hours 10 minutes
Total cost of R101:	£711,595 (including modifications)

The total cost of the R101 project 1924–30, including design and construction costs, erection of bases, masts and sheds at home and abroad at the height of the Depression was £1,925,835. In today's terms that would probably be in excess of £60 million.

APPENDIX 2

Passenger and Crew List on Board R101
4/5 October 1930

Passengers

1. Brigadier-General, The Right Hon. Lord Thomson of Cardington (HM Secretary of State for Air) – killed; not identified.
2. Air Vice-Marshal Sir W. Sefton Brancker (Director of Civil Aviation) – killed; identified on return to London.
3. Major Percy Bishop (Chief Inspector AID) – killed; not identified.
4. Squadron Leader W. Palstra RAAF (representing the Australian Government) – killed; not identified.
5. Squadron Leader W. O'Neill (Deputy Director of Civil Aviation, India) – killed; identified on return to London.
6. Mr James Buck, Lord Thomson's valet – killed; identified on return to London.

Officials of the Royal Airship Works, Cardington

7. Wing Commander R.B.B. Colmore (DAD) – killed; identified on return to London.
8. Major G.H. Scott (ADAD Flying) – killed; not identified.
9. Lt.Col. V.C. Richmond (ADAD Technical) – killed; identified on return to London.
10. Squadron Leader F.M. Rope (Assistant to DAD Technical) – killed; identified on return to London.
11. Mr Alexander Bushfield, AID – killed; identified on return to London.
12. Mr A.H. Leech, Foreman Engineer Cardington – survivor.

Officers of R101

13. Flight Lieutenant H. Carmichael Irwin (Captain) – killed; identified on return to London.
14. Squadron Leader E.L. Johnston (Navigator) – killed; not identified.
15. Lt-Commander N.G. Atherstone (First Officer) – killed; identified on return to London.
16. Flying Officer M.H. Steff (Second Officer) – killed; not identified.
17. Mr M.A. Giblett (Chief Meteorological Officer) – killed; identified on return to London.

Petty Officers and Charge Hands

18. G.W. Hunt (Chief Coxswain) – killed; not identified.
19. W.R. Gent (Chief Engineer) – killed; identified on return to London.
20. G.W. Short (Charge-Hand Engineer) – killed; not identified.
21. S.E. Scott (Charge-Hand Engineer) – killed; identified at Allonne.
22. T. Key (Charge-Hand Engineer) – killed; not identified.
23. S.T. Keeley (Chief Wireless Operator) – killed; not identified.
24. A.H. Savidge (Chief Steward) – killed; not identified.

Crew Members

25. Flight-Sergeant W.A. Potter (Assistant Coxswain) – killed; identified at Allonne.
26. L.F. Oughton (Assistant Coxswain) – killed; identified on return to London.
27. C.H. Mason (Assistant Coxswain) – killed; not identified.
28. M.G. Rampton (Assistant Coxswain) – killed; identified on return to London.
29. H.E. Ford (Assistant Coxswain) – killed; not identified.
30. P.A. Foster (Assistant Coxswain) – killed; not identified.
31. F.G. Rudd (Rigger) – killed; identified at Allonne.
32. C.F. Taylor (Rigger) – killed; identified on return to London.
33. A.W.J. Norcott (Rigger) – killed; not identified.
34. A.J. Richardson (Rigger) – killed; identified on return to London.
35. W.G. Radcliffe (Rigger) – survived, but died at Beauvais on October 6th.
36. S. Church (Rigger) – survived, but died at Beauvais on October 8th.
37. R. Blake (Engineer) – killed; identified at Allonne.
38. C.A. Burton (Engineer) – killed; identified on return to London.
39. C.J. Fergusson (Engineer) – killed; not identified.
40. A.C. Hastings (Engineer) – killed; not identified.
41. W.H. King (Engineer) – killed; identified on return to London.
42. M.F. Littlekitt (Engineer) No. 1 car – killed; not identified.
43. W. Moule (Engineer) No. 2 car – killed; identified on return to London.
44. A.H. Watkins (Engineer) – killed; not identified.
45. A.V. Bell (Engineer) No. 5 car – survivor.
46. J.H. Binks (Engineer) No. 5 car – survivor.
47. A.J. Cook (Engineer) No. 4 car – survivor.
48. V. Savory (Engineer) No. 3 car – survivor.
49. G.H. Atkins (Wireless Operator) – killed; identified on return to London.
50. F. Elliott (Wireless Operator) – killed; identified on return to London.
51. A. Disley (Wireless Operator/Electrician) – survivor.
52. F. Hodnett (*aka* J. Curran) (Assistant Steward) – killed; not identified.
53. E.A. Graham (Cook) – killed; not identified.
54. T.W. Megginson (Galley Boy) – killed, not identified.

Select Bibliography

Chamberlain, Geoffrey, *Airships – Cardington*, Terence Dalton 1991
Johnston, E.A., *Airship Navigator*, Skyline 1994
Leasor, James, *The Millionth Chance*, Hamish Hamilton 1957
Masefield, Sir Peter G., *To Ride the Storm*, William Kimber 1982
Wattebled, Laurent, *La Catastrophe du 'R-101'*, Beauvais 1990
Dirigible, House Journal of the Airship Heritage Trust 1991 to date
Flight, Illustrated London News, etc. various, 1928–31

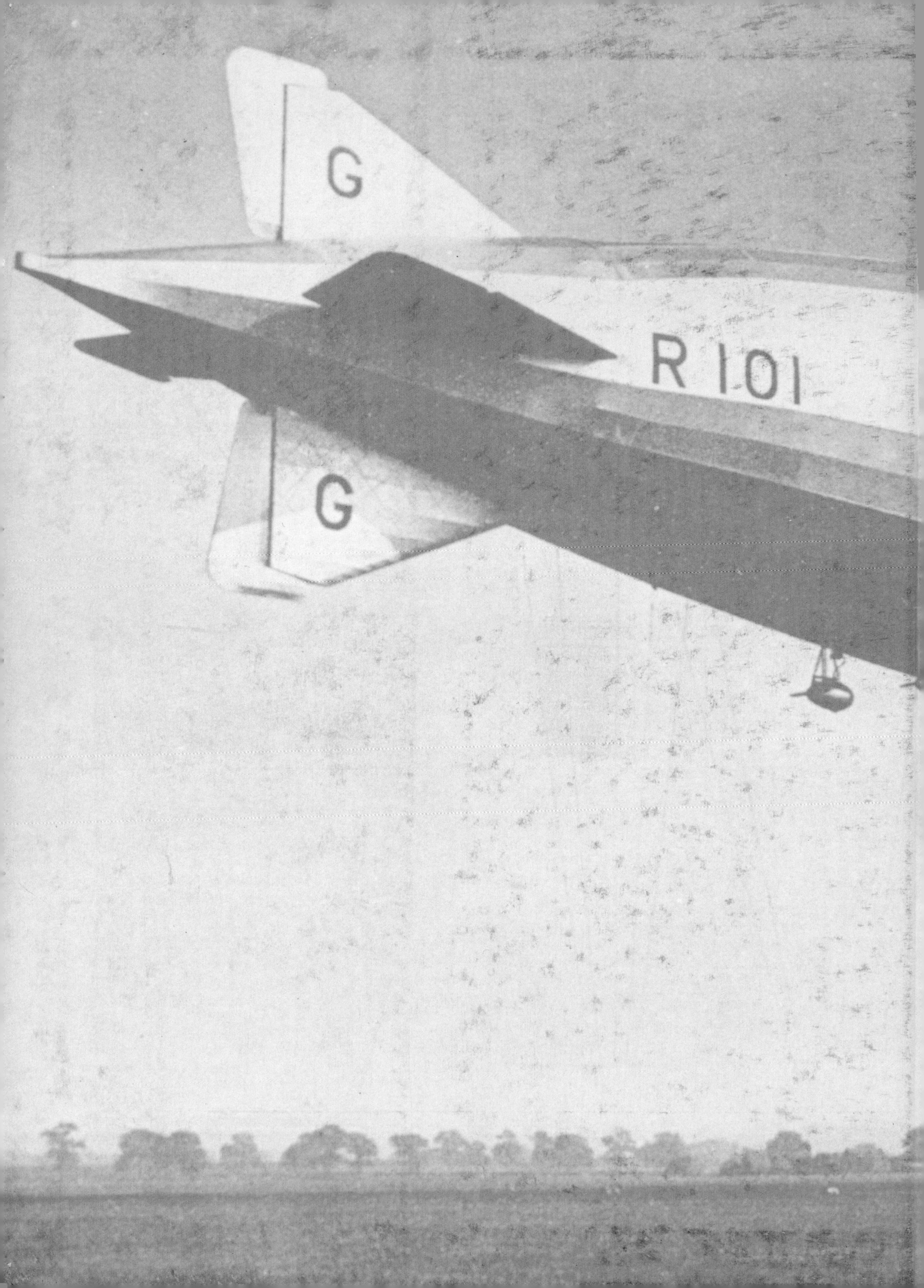
G
R101
G